MW01292652

From a very young age, I remember being fascinated with the photo albums that my grandmother kept on the top shelf of the closet of one of her guest bedrooms. I would open that wooden door, and I remember being flooded with a very distinct smell. Not a bad smell, just a....*scent*. It could've been mothballs, but whatever it was, I remember I would instantly feel a pang of familiarity and excitement as I reached up to grab as many photo albums as my little hands could wrap themselves around, while not letting them completely fall over the top of my head and onto the hardwood floors to cause a big ruckus, thereby causing an adult to come in and see what I was up to.

I would make myself comfortable on the old twin bed, which I recall was always rock hard and had starched sheets with brightly colored flowers on them. That particular room had a big window that looked out into my grandmother's back yard, which was always busy with birds, squirrels and blooming flowers. Next to that bed was a small desk that had one of the first Apple computers of the mid 1980s—the tiny ones with the black screens and neon green letters. There was a bright yellow school room chair that sat at that little desk. It's strange what your mind remembers from a very early age.

I would open the albums, staring at them page by page as I had done so many times before, letting myself be transported to a different world, made all the more fascinating because of the fact that it was *real.* Sometimes I would peel back the cellophane page cover and peel off the photo from the sticky page to get a closer look at the details. These weren't photos of random people in a history book; they were photos of my family, my bloodline. Each time I would scan the old photographs of my maternal grandmother and grandfather in the early

1940s—some before they were married, some after they were married, and all before having children. I would scan for any details that would give my wildly intrigued brain more of a glimpse into the world that had come before my mother, and long before me; whether it was a detail on a house, a particular button or pin on a blouse, a scuff on a shoe, a license plate on a car, a ring on a finger, or even chipped nail polish on said finger—I would sit there trying to squeeze the marrow out of these historic photographs; snapshots of time gone by and of a world that I would never know.

In full disclosure, when I was about nine or ten years old, I was a total snoop. I would look in dresser drawers, in cabinets, anything that would open. I never stole anything; I was just nosy—*curious* sounds better. And one particular day when I was around eight or nine years old, I was peeking into the top drawer of my grandmother's dresser in her other guest room; the room we affectionately called "The Blue Room." It was called that because the furniture was a distressed baby blue, and the shag carpeting was a horrific melting pot of various shades of blue, green and lavender—I'm sure decades before it was absolutely in style.

The blue and lavender floral bedspread—which was itchier than steel wool-- matched that blue and lavender carpet. My cousin, Danielle, and I loved that room because of the vanity with the big circle mirror. We would sit there for hours, putting on makeup we likely bought with our allowance at Wal-Mart or the Dollar Tree. I'm sure if a fly could've been on the walls of that blue room, oh the stories it would've heard!

But I digress. On this particular day, I was alone and being nosy. I opened the top drawer of the big dresser and started picking through items. There I found several items that, upon first glance, I could tell belonged to my grandfather. One dark-colored, leather case caught my eye first, and I picked it up and examined it. The leather on the outside was worn and no longer shiny.

In a split second, my little hands opened that case. In that case was a Purple Heart. *A **Purple Heart**.* I felt my stomach turn a little bit, and a pang of adrenaline washed through my entire body, from my heart, down to my feet and back up through my arms to my head. My heart began pounding—the kind of adrenaline shock that leaves you a little shaky and cold-sweaty. I may have been young, but I knew what a Purple Heart meant if someone received one—it meant they had been wounded in battle. I had never heard of this in our family before. I never knew anyone fought in a war. How did I not know this? I shook my head and set the case aside ever so gently—almost as if it contained something tiny and alive—and I continued digging.

I found photographs, the black and white ones that dated themselves with the ruffled edges; most were of my grandmother with my grandfather—very early in their relationship. At this point, I wasn't sure if they were married or just dating…whenever it was, they looked so young! As a child, to see your grandparents resemble the same face they have now, but minus the years and life lived, to see them still as kids themselves in their early 20s, at the time—it was something that my mind could barely wrap itself around. And they looked so happy with each other.

Then I found postcards, various letters and pieces of paper that looked foreign to me, but I that I eventually realized were telegrams. They were yellow and aged and had that distinct old paper smell. They had been folded and unfolded many times and were worn and somewhat ragged around the edges.

The letters were in perfect black ink block letters from a typewriter. Some were addressed from the War Department in Washington D.C., while some were from the Headquarters for Army Services, also from Washington D.C., and several were from a company in St. Louis, Missouri called Rice-Stix. (*I would later learn more about this company and what it meant to my grandmother and grandfather.*)

I was sucked in. I can't remember how many hours passed in that one sitting; reading and taking in as much as I could understand as a ten year old, who just moments before discovering this treasure trove was probably more concerned with the latest boy band I was listening to at the time, with tears welling up at some points and holding my breath at other points. There was so much information that had not been talked about—or had it been mentioned and I just wasn't old enough to listen or understand? Our family wasn't one that swept things under the rug that I was aware of. I was now seeing both my grandmother and my grandfather in a whole new light. I remember putting everything away—careful to place it all back in its perfect place so my discovery wouldn't be noticed--and emerging from that room...*different*. After that day, every time I was at my grandmother's house, which was often, I would quietly slither into that guest bedroom, get those photo albums or look at the letters and postcards; I was inexplicably drawn to them. I couldn't get enough of them.

While my cousins were more concerned with who got to spin the wheel on the old Apple computer game *Wheel of Fortune*, I would gravitate toward that box of letters, and I would hold them between my fingers and smell them. They had that "old paper" smell that you would find in a dusty attic or in the deep bowels of an old library. I would imagine what it was like so many years before; for my grandmother to hold those letters in her hands as they were delivered to her when she was younger than I am now. I was beyond intrigued, I was *infatuated* and borderline obsessed. I would remain this way throughout the rest of my years in school studying World War II and learning as much as my teenage brain could absorb about what that time meant for us as a country, and for my grandmother as a young war wife.

I never pried or asked questions about this time for her. To my knowledge, no one did. Years down the road, my grandmother eventually put together a booklet of articles, letters, photos, badges; everything I had come across so many years ago and gave a copy to each of her children so they would have all of their father's history at their fingertips as well. His story lives on in the articles and letters, but *her story* is still in her mind and in her heart, until now—or as much as she was willing to let me have. Some of the names and minor details have been changed, and I'm going off of what my grandmother has told me from what her mind recalls—sometimes it seems she recalls events of more than seventy years ago better than events happening around her today.

I suppose when you are 96, that is both a blessing and a curse. I have asked numerous questions to unearth as much of her personal memory as possible regarding this time in her life, and I have used all of the letters, telegrams, and newspaper articles pertinent specifically to my grandfather. I have developed a story around the facts that were presented to me. This is a novel based on her incredible true story.

This is a story about resilience. This is a story of how strong the human heart can be under fear and uncertainty, not to mention under the weight of a world war. This is the story of a miracle for one woman and a timeless love story. This is a story based on true events that were lived, breathed, suffered and survived.

This is the story of an incredible woman's unlikely journey through early life during the Depression, a childhood in poverty, being a war wife, then almost a war widow, then a wife…and a mother…and a successful teacher and world traveler.

This is the story of my grandmother, Helen B. Little. To her many grandchildren and even more great grandchildren, she goes by "Memaw." She is the matriarch of my mother's side of the family, and she is often referred to as a saint. We always say she has a "straight line to Jesus" for when her time comes. At the time of printing, I am 35 and she is 96. Why I felt a stirring in the pit of my soul to write this at this point in my life and hers, I do not know.

Perhaps it is the realization that we may not have as many years left with her as we think we do. She has always been seemingly invincible to us. When she was 80, she said with conviction that she did not hope to live to 90, and that "there was no reason to." Well, that birthday has come and gone. Her body is thin and not as agile as it once was; but her heart is mighty, and her brain is as sharp as the razor tongue she can often surprise you with….I think we can all agree that when you're 96, you can say whatever you damn well please, and she holds up this truth much to our great humor most of the time.

This is a story that deserved to be put on paper, if for no one else other than our family. For without this story, my family and I would simply cease to exist.

It is my hope that others will read this and take an interest in their own family's stories, roots and history. Our grandparents are gifts. They were of a different time and a different era. Boys would become men much faster than they planned. Many of those men would not return home.

My grandfather was almost one of them. In fact, it was a very real possibility that he may not be coming home ever again—my grandmother was left with the thought of facing life without him. Her dreams of marriage and a family were being taken from her before they ever really began—or so she thought. Her story and life are so remarkable that it was easy for my imagination to take flight and fill in some gaps that were left by the hands of time.

This is her story of that snapshot in time that shaped the rest of her beautiful life.

~For Memaw & Pepaw~

This is a love letter to the grandmother I admire more than words can do justice; for her courage, her tenacity and her unwavering strength in her 96 years and counting, and to the grandfather I wish I had known for more than four years of my life— thank you for your service and your sacrifice. Thank you for being the One for my grandmother and for helping to shape her life as well as the life of our whole family. Writing this book has allowed me a glimpse into your life, into your world that I would have never known, and even though it is heartbreaking to finish this and say goodbye to you, I will hold you in my heart forever.

A Dream Realized

Commencement 1974; Southeast Missouri State University; Cape Girardeau, Missouri

"Helen B. Little," University President Mark F. Scully, called from behind the wooden podium. With one foot in front of the other, Helen made her way to the center of the stage to receive a piece of paper that let the world know that she had earned her Master's Degree. *A Master of Arts in education,* to be exact. She was almost 53 years old, standing in a sea of graduates, most of which were approximately 25 years younger than her. She extended her right hand to shake the hand of President Scully, and her left hand grasped the piece of paper tightly. She glanced out into the crowd, which included her husband John and five of her six children—her oldest son, Joe, had moved out of state with his family.

"How did I get here?" she thought silently to herself. It wasn't a *bad* feeling; quite the contrary…it was the *best* feeling. This was a different feeling—overwhelmingly joyous and proud. She received her Bachelor of Science in elementary education in 1968 after more than 40 years from finishing her first year of college. She remembered being happy then, but knew she had to do more. She was going to be entering the workforce much later than most teachers typically do, and she needed as much education under her belt as possible to walk away with the best retirement possible—and at 53 years old, that wasn't a terribly far off thought.

Always a strong woman, never faltering under pressure, keeping her chin high in good times and bad, Helen knew exactly how she got to this point, on this stage, with this evidence of higher education in her hand.

Through sheer determination, hard work and a supportive husband, that's how. A feeling of pure pride welled up in her in that moment, and she closed her eyes for a split second vowing to never forget this picture in time—this moment that seemed so far out of reach for so long. After all, it had been more than *40 years* since she finished her first year of college. So much life was ahead of her back then that she wasn't even aware of; twists and turns that she could've never anticipated.

In this split second, as she stared at the strong and proud face of her husband John, they locked eyes and they both knew something the rest of the people in that hot auditorium did not; this moment almost wasn't possible. This *life* Helen knew and loved almost wouldn't happen. And those six children, who weren't so little anymore, ranging in ages from 16 to 32, they were so close to not existing. As she made her way across the stage and back to her seat, the rest of the ceremony would be a blur, her mind drifted back—back to what would be the beginning of her incredible and unlikely journey.

.

A Humble Beginning

It was May 1940. The early summer sun was beating down on Helen, as she stared out the passenger side window of a rusty 1937 Ford. With Julia, her friend from high school, in the driver's seat chattering on about her summer plans, Helen was free to let her mind roam on what may lie ahead for her future. She was returning to Millwood, Missouri after completing a year of school at Kirksville College in Kirksville, Missouri; majoring in education. After completing high school in Silex, Missouri, Helen was granted a scholarship for one year of college. One year of college wasn't the same as four years, nor was it enough to say you possessed a degree or expertise in anything, but it was *something*—for a woman in the early 1940s, in rural Missouri—it was a lot in fact.

Most people, not just women, who had grown up during the Depression, or in the immediate aftermath did not finish but a few years of elementary school. Families needed all the help they could get with duties on the farm or in the household just to make ends meet and keep food on the table. In rural Missouri, only one male per household was permitted to work on the farm full time. If there were multiple boys in the family, they would each work half-time along with their father. The reason for this was so that if there were any injuries or casualties, the entire work-force of a family wouldn't be wiped out at once.

Girls would often be needed inside the home to help tend to the cooking, cleaning, making clothes, raising chickens and growing vegetables on the farm, caring for younger siblings, etc. To be able to go to school in those days for any length of time was more of a luxury than anything; although as is typical of children of any age or time period, going to school wasn't most kids' favorite pastime.

Barbara Helen Clem (she always went by Helen) grew up in Millwood to a mother, Opal, who kept the family running from inside the home. Her father, Russell, although he meant well, was a fan of the drink and had a hard time holding down a farming job, but he worked hard and managed to keep his family fed and clothed. Helen and her five sisters and two brothers would be moved almost every year, it seemed, from one farm to the next. Her father always managed to get the next job; he just wasn't great at *keeping* the job. Out of the 50 or so people in Millwood when Helen was growing up, her family was by far the poorest. It wasn't something she was always acutely aware of though—kids in school didn't make fun of her family or the fact that her mother made all of her and her sisters' clothes from flour sacks because they couldn't afford fabric. The family's old Ford carried Helen, her mother and siblings to and from St. Alphonsus Catholic Church every Sunday. Her father was not a churchgoer.

Having a car was a blessing back then, however that old Ford wasn't built to go up the steep hills which had to be navigated to get to the church, so when they approached a hill, Helen's oldest brother just turned that old car around and they went up those hills backwards. Every. Single. Sunday. To this day, Helen has no idea why it had more force going backwards than forward; but it did, and that's something that she remembers vividly and always with a laugh. The town folks would get together to butcher the animals raised on the farms for their meat, and Helen, with her mother and sisters, would tend to the chickens and the vegetables in the garden. Her mother would take the eggs and occasionally a chicken to the store and sell them for other essentials that the family needed. It was a tough way to live, but when you don't know any other way to live, you make it work and it didn't seem so bad. From the time she was five years old until she was 14, Helen and her sisters walked the dusty three miles one way to and from their elementary school. The walk to and from school was brutal almost year-round, except for the brief respite that fall and spring would bring. The late August mid-Missouri air was so thick you could cut it with a knife while trying not to choke on it. She and her sisters would be sweaty messes before even entering the schoolhouse at the beginning of a new year. The winters offered no remorse either, for the girls would often dodge sleet and stinging winds on that same walk that nearly suffocated them months before. Regardless of the weather or time of year, Helen would find herself at home inside a school room. While most kids hated going to school at that age, she knew what a privilege it was. She worked very hard and she excelled.

When high school approached, Helen and her older sister, Arlene, attended school in the neighboring town of Silex, Missouri. Since she didn't have her own car, Helen had to hitch a ride with friends for the first two years. For a while, the neighbor boy, Artie Langenecker, would give the girls a ride. Artie had the most flaming red hair Helen had ever seen on a boy, and she often found herself stifling laughter every time that red head came bouncing out the front door each morning. He was a goofy looking kid, but nice enough.

Rumor had it that he had a thing for Helen. That was always an inside joke between Helen and Arlene that could get the girls giggling for hours when they got to talking about the thought of Helen dating *Artie Langenecker*. She didn't seem to care or have mutual thoughts whatsoever…she was just grateful for the ride every day. Occasionally she wonders where that boy ever ended up in life.

The last two years of high school she lived with a friend in Silex for a small fee—which she paid for by working in the high school library a few hours after school each day. She liked working in the library. It was quiet. It was peaceful. Books opened her mind up to the big world outside the small, poor bubble that was Millwood, Missouri. She tried to read as much as she could in between her regular schoolwork. This is where the spark for the thought of possibly becoming a teacher one day ignited in her soul. Helen knew that if she could absorb everything she could in high school, college may not be such a distant dream, and then she could teach for a living.

She could inspire children to think outside their immediate surroundings and show them that a big and exciting world awaited them. This was her calling—she could feel it.

Helen studied hard and would go on to become the Valedictorian of her high school class. This would earn her the only scholarship available—one year to Kirksville College, where she would excel and take in everything she possibly could in the field of education and how to be a proper teacher to children.

Now that year was up, and Helen was headed back to Millwood. Back to the dusty old farm town she called home only a few years before. She was going to be a teacher.

The Millwood public school was a one room, run-down, dilapidated school house that was on the brink of closing. None of that mattered to Helen nor did it deter her. She was realizing her dream. She was going to be a teacher. Nor did it matter that in her first year of teaching she only had three students. *Three students.*

Those three students were going to be the best and brightest three students that they could possibly be. She was going to be the one to inspire them.

Helen's daydreaming came to a literal halt when Julia cut the turn into Helen's family's drive a little too tight, jolting her back to reality. It was then that Helen realized Julia had been talking the entire drive and Helen hadn't heard a word she'd said.

Julia didn't seem to realize or mind—she was like that—she could talk to a brick wall. She wasn't the most serious of people; she was bubbly and chatty and often wore Helen out. She wished Helen a good summer and the girls agreed they would catch up in a few weeks. The last year had seemed like a blur. Helen knew she had grown up as a woman, felt proud of her college accomplishment and was confident in her teaching abilities. It was time to get to work.

The following Monday, Helen made her way into the dilapidated school house and stood in front of her three less-than-enthusiastic students. Two little boys, who looked like they got into a fight with one another on the way to school—dirty and disheveled and one was sporting a black eye that was beginning to show up very clearly.

The little girl reminded Helen of herself at that young age. She was in a patchwork flour sack dress. Her hair was tied into two braids on either side and her mother had put two pieces of package twine around them in little bows. She seemed shy and not too sure about being in this room with the two boys. The two boys were six years old and the little girl was seven years old. "Lord give me strength," Helen thought to herself as she grasped at the cross she wore on a gold chain around her neck.

She knew she had her work cut out for her, even with such a small number of students. One would think a larger class would be more intimidating, but Helen would've preferred more kids.

This was far more daunting—with those three sets of eyes just staring up at her. But, never one to shy away from a challenge, Helen got to personally know her students, developed a curriculum that would allow them to be individuals, yet thrive as a group. They would learn to think outside the box and find creative ways to solve problems. After a few weeks Helen began to settle into the position and after only a few months, she knew this was her calling. She was going to be a teacher for the rest of her life. She had no way of knowing how she would get there—she just knew she would…someday.

On a cool Sunday morning in early fall, Helen made her way into St. Alphonsus Catholic Church, just as she had every Sunday. The sun was shining just in a way that everything had that sort of idyllic golden hue to it; the early stages of the red and orange colors in the trees were beginning to show. The air had that early fall crisp feel to it, and the thick summer air had faded away for good, at least until next summer. The new coolness in the air gave her a little more pep in her step. She felt like this often around the turn of the seasons. It felt like a new beginning. This day felt different.

She could tell that great things were on the horizon for her, and she felt optimistic, happy and peaceful.

Helen practically skipped her way into the sanctuary and into one of the hard wooden pews.

After the first hymn, she happened to glance around to see who was there on this particular Sunday, and a tall, dark haired young man caught her attention. He was handsome. He had wavy brown hair, blue eyes and thin lips that made for the sweetest hint of a smile. He wore thin wire-rimmed glasses, which made him look smart. He was dressed very nice, sharp and well put together. Although she didn't know him personally, she recognized him as John Little. He was a few years older than her. His family had a very nice home right next to the church and his father had a decent job working for a company that supervised farm help. When you come from a town of about 50 people, it was extremely rare to not know of someone, even if you didn't know them personally. Complete strangers were sniffed out pretty quickly in Millwood by the few women who were the village voices, and those strangers wouldn't be strangers for too long. John looked over and caught her eye with a grin that would be burned into her memory forever. After exchanging some glances during the mass, Helen made her way out of the church and onto the front steps, half hoping to see John again, and half feeling ridiculous for thinking like a little schoolgirl.

She was fastening the buttons on her jacket when she looked up and saw him walking right toward her. Her heart skipped a beat, and she felt her face begin to flush as he approached her.

By now the butterflies in her stomach had turned into giant birds flapping their wings obnoxiously. She silently told herself to get it together. *This was not her.* She did not behave like a giddy schoolgirl. She was a professional teacher, after all. She smoothed out her jacket, took a deep breath, looked up and smiled. This handsome man looked right at her and said "Hi, I'm John Little" with a very polite but confident voice. Helen held out her hand and introduced herself as well—immediately embarrassed at the girly tone in her voice. She cleared her throat and composed herself. They made some small chit-chat as they strolled around the grounds by the church and then he asked her if she would be interested in going to a dance with him the next weekend. She thought that sounded like a fine idea.

And with that, she turned on her heels and headed home—she might as well have been floating on a cloud. She barely felt her feet hit the ground with each step and there was a smile on her face that wouldn't be fading anytime soon. Helen was sure this was the man she would spend the rest of her life with. Something inside her told her that he was special—and she knew she would follow him to the ends of the earth if she needed to. John Joseph Little was her person.

John came from a nice family—a wealthy family, by rural Missouri standards—which wouldn't amount to much by the wealthy standards of some of the rich families in the rest of the United States at that time. Although he didn't go school past the sixth grade, he began working with his father at a young age on farms and then with his father's farm supervising business. He had a hard, honest work ethic, and he caught on fast. The fact that he didn't have an education past grade school didn't seem to matter; he had a good business brain, and it served him well then and would continue to serve him well in the future.

John had two sisters and two brothers, and he was in the middle of them. They were definitely considered an affluent family in Millwood.

Dating in Millwood, Missouri in the late 1930s and early 1940s wasn't exactly what dating looked like anywhere else in the United States, or at least in bigger cities. There were no movie theatres to go to, no drive-ins to meet up with friends and no real restaurants to sit across from one another and talk over a meal in an intimate setting while being waited on.

The dating "scene" in Millwood consisted of going to dances, usually at the church, being with each other and friends at town or church picnics or just getting to know one another by having meals with each other's families in their homes.

After that first dance at St. Alphonsus, Helen and John were inseparable. Their personalities were perfectly complimentary of one another. She was a bit of an unexpected sparkplug—quiet but very quick to supply a witty remark or comeback—she had a sly sense of humor that John found irresistible. He was stoic and quiet most of the time; but he would come out of his shell with a group of friends, and he had a quiet, sweet sense of humor. They meshed together perfectly, and Helen couldn't believe her luck.

After several of months dating, they were married on July 19, 1941. Helen's older sister, Arlene, picked out and paid for her wedding dress. Her dress was off-white silk with pearl buttons that decorated the neckline and lined the belt around her waist. She wore white gloves and a hat, which was very common for ladies in 1941. He wore a dashing suit and tie with white dress shoes. Helen thought he was the most handsome creature she had ever laid eyes on. They had a small wedding with Arlene and John's brother, Marion, standing in as Maid of Honor and Best Man respectively. After the ceremony, Helen's mom hosted a fried chicken dinner with the immediate families of both sides.

Love and laughter hung in the air in Millwood, Missouri that night.

The thick late summer air hugged the newlyweds and their families as they chatted and mingled amongst each other.

Music was playing, and some were dancing; all were smiling and enjoying the occasion and the company. Fireflies dotted the summer night sky, cicadas sang their lullabies in the background, and Helen took it all in and wanted this feeling to last forever. John had taken a seat on the back steps of the house, and Helen joined him. She grasped John's hand, looked into his beautiful eyes, and thanked God silently in her heart for the gift of this man that she would now be spending her life with.

"Thank you God, for John Joseph Little, my *husband*," she said in her heart. He looked back at her and, with that sweet smile and a wink, she knew he felt the same for her.

John had a wife to support now, so he quickly got a
job in Warrenton, Missouri, where he worked for a
manufacturing plant during the day while Helen
helped set up their home in an upstairs apartment
that had one bedroom, a kitchen and not much else.
Helen hated to leave her new teaching career
behind; however, she was going to follow John
anywhere. They made the best of less-than-
desirable housing and enjoyed their time as
newlyweds. They would move on to Saint Louis
when he got a better job offer at a company called
Rice-Stix, which was a manufacturing plant that
produced, among other items, luggage and clothing.
During this time, most of the country was in
waiting. Pearl Harbor had happened and men were
being required to enlist into the armed forces for
inevitable deployment to active duty.

Soon enough, John's time came to enlist and off they went to their first stationing, which was at Camp McCoy in Wisconsin. Of course, Helen was bothered by the thought of her new husband having to enlist and go off into this world war for God knows how long, but she wouldn't show it—these were the times they were living in, and she accepted the fact that this is just how things were going to be. She was raised to be strong and steady. She would support her husband with her head held high, and she wouldn't be one of those wives who cried and carried on in agony while waiting for their husbands to come home. Helen had a home to maintain and a job to do, and she was going to do it to the very best of her ability. She was not one to ever sit around and sulk about anything, and she certainly wasn't going to start with that nonsense now. When she took the vows 'in good times and in bad', she meant it. John wasn't even deployed into the war yet…he was in training, but Helen knew that the time would come when his name would be called, and he would have to go into the unknown. He would be sent into the eye of the storm at some point; that was just a fact. She knew the risks, but they seemed so foreign and far away at this point. Right now, she and John were simply just doing their jobs—and loving life as newlyweds in the meantime.

John would eventually be stationed at Camp Tyson in Paris, Tennessee. During this time, while John was preparing to go to war, Helen worked various office jobs that were considered high level since she had gone to high school and had some college education. It wasn't uncommon for the women then to have what were deemed "lower level" jobs that were more manual labor "grunt work" rather than office work. Helen worked in various rationing office jobs—one for tires, then one for sugar. The sugar ration was the bane of most war wives' existence, aside from their men being gone, of course. Back then, there were no sugar substitutes like there are today and people certainly didn't shun white cane sugar like they do today.

Cane sugar was a staple in the American household. It was being rationed in order to serve the forces first. Most American families got a "ration coupon" to use at the grocery store in order to buy the items, including sugar, which had been put on a ration list.

During this time at Camp Tyson, Helen obtained her driver's license, which was also very rare for a woman to have during this time. Because she could drive, she became the person who took their friends—two other military couples: Phillip and Margaret, and Michael and Jane—to and from Camp Tyson, home to St. Louis and back again when they had free weekends or time off. Usually it was just the women on these trips since the men were in constant training and worked very long hours seven days a week.

Since Helen was the only one with a driver's license, she was always the driver. It was during these drives that her mind would shift to the future. How long would this war go on? Where would they end up? Where would he be sent? How long would he be gone? Would he even come back? "Stop it Helen," she would silently whisper to herself. "Of course he will come home, he has to." These were the questions that would bubble up in her mind while she was in a trance on the road, oblivious to the conversations between her friends who sat in the back seat.

Helen didn't understand how Margaret and Jane could just sit there and gossip about the latest "junk news" of the day. They would somehow obtain copies of fashion magazines, LIFE Magazine was a popular one back then, and they would sit and flip through those pages and discuss the fashions and latest gossip, as if there were no war going on at all. Helen's thoughts would periodically be interrupted by the shrill sound of cackling laughter coming from the back seat—no doubt Margaret, the highly inappropriate one of the bunch—had told an offensive joke, and Jane had a laugh so loud and so high-pitched that Helen often thought if she laughed any louder, the windows on the car would blow out. She often felt bad that she didn't join in their banter more.

Helen had a sense of humor; in fact, she thought Margaret was hilarious most of the time. She was great comic relief and often reminded her of her sister, Arlene, whom she missed greatly while on the road with John.

But on the drives to and from St. Louis, Helen just didn't feel like cutting up. She would think about John and what their future was going to look like. Everything was just so uncertain. Little did she know, this was only the beginning of the uncertainty that was going to flood Helen's life soon enough.

Hitting a pothole in the road would snap Helen out of that dark hole of worry, and she would force a smile and attempt to join back in the conversation.

Helen was constantly busy with work and various other duties, and she loved that. She felt like she was making a difference. She felt needed. Staying busy in the office was the only thing keeping her mind off the fact that inevitably her beloved John was going to go to war. The world didn't stop for any of the other women affected by their husbands going to war, and it certainly wasn't going to stop for Helen either.

It was in the quiet moments of the early evening when John would be finishing dinner across the table from her, that she would steal a glance—his kind eyes tired from a long day of training—and he would smile back at her, knowing what was on her mind. He would try to reassure her with a wink and a grin, which he had been doing since their wedding day, which also masked any worry he was undoubtedly feeling on the inside.

Helen would hold on to these moments as long as she possibly could; burning his smile into her brain, until John received orders to be shipped out.

On November 28, 1942, John was officially inducted into the United States Armed Forces, and on December 5, 1942, he officially began his active duty as a soldier. He would be sent with the first wave of D-Day invaders to Normandy. And with this, Helen's "new normal" began.

With John gone to war, Helen needed a more stable place, to be close to family and to live where she could afford to pay rent without John present. She and her sister Arlene rented an apartment at 5838 Enright Avenue in St. Louis, and she took a job working for CV Mosby Medical Publishing, a company that published medical books. She would help run the office, which again, was a pretty substantial job for a woman during this time.

Helen liked being in the familiar setting of books all day long. Medical books weren't exactly fascinating to her, but it was at least productive work. This work was tedious but it kept her mind from wandering. It kept the fear of the unknown from creeping in, causing anxiety to well up. Although processing orders for books would at times get tedious, and she could feel her brain start to get the better of her occasionally, she would have to snap out of it, pay attention to the job she was doing and push those thoughts out of her mind.

She thought about all of those housewives who had to stay at home with children all day and all night. Being a housewife was no easy task, she fully realized, but having to be surrounded by photos and memories and tend to children, all while being terrified about their husbands' well-being off in some foreign land without being able to get away from it all—that sounded miserable she thought. At least she had a place to get up and go to every morning and a task to focus on for eight hours a day, five days a week.

It wasn't until nighttime when she would finally allow her mind to wander. There was really no way to stop it. The world had quieted down around her, and she would lay in bed, keeping John's space on the other side of the bed open, waiting for him. It was in those quiet moments, while waiting for her brain to shut down enough to fall asleep that she would wonder where he was in the world right this moment, and of course she wondered *how* he was.

She would hope and pray that he was safe and being fed enough.

She wondered if he was scared or if he felt confident in the training he received so briefly before shipping out. She would get letters here and there from him letting her know at least that he was alive and doing the tasks he was trained to do. However, she got the sense that there was more he wasn't telling her; that he was seeing things he didn't want her to have to imagine. It was as if she had hit a wall with him. He was telling her what she wanted to hear and no more, no less. The letters were short, formal and to the point. Helen knew John missed her; there was no question about that. But the letters were vague and cryptic, and there was a sizeable time gap from when he sent the letters to when she actually received them…sometimes weeks had already passed.

Stories flooded the newspapers about casualties, Germans taking wounded soldiers as prisoners of war—all of it was horrifying to Helen as she would read what she could, and then she would fold up the paper, choosing to believe the best and carry on with her day. It all just seemed so…far away. It was hard to envision John being on the other side of the world dealing with this war. Sometimes she would close her eyes and it would just seem as though he were gone for the day—until the relentless glare of nighttime came and reality struck again. Helen didn't hear much from him, but she knew enough to know that no news was good news...*usually*. No member of the armed forces had shown up on her doorstep yet, so that was a positive. Every day that went by without that happening was a day closer to John hopefully coming home.

Simple as that, she would remind herself. He does his job over there, and he comes home. End of story. And with that thought in her head, she would fall asleep, wake up again and go about her day.

Stalag 3C. According to the dictionary, a *Stalag* is a noun. Anyone who was actually held in a stalag might have referred to it as hell; it's hard to say since most of the soldiers held during this time have long since passed away. A stalag was a German prison camp in World War II, especially for noncommissioned officers and privates. There were various stalags all over Germany during this time. Stalag 3C would eventually be a term Helen would come to know more about than she had ever hoped. She would come to *detest* the term Stalag 3C, for it was within these cold, heartless, violent prison walls that her whole future came close to never existing. The man she loved more than she knew she was capable of loving could've lost his life….and the future children she wanted to have with John, her hopes of being a teacher—all of that was almost taken from her with the words Stalag 3C.

There are several websites that give some insight into the stalags of WWII, but overall there is not much information about the specifics of these camps. According to information found on www.allstalags.com, "Stalag 3C was a German Army Second World War POW camp for allied soldiers. It was located on a plain near the village of Alt Drewitz bei Kustrin in the Neumark of the state of Brandenburg (present day Drzewice, Kostrzyn and Odra, Poland), about 80km east of Berlin. In June 1940, the camp was established 6km from Kustrin for Belgian and French prisoners from the Battle of France. In July 1941, Soviet prisoners taken during Operation Barbarossa arrived.

They were held in separate facilities, and according to records, suffered severe conditions and starvation. They were not given the humane treatment required by the Third Geneva Convention. Thousands died from starvation and disease. In September 1943 Italians who had been interned because of the Italian Armistice arrived. September 1944, the first Americans arrived. In December 1944, more American prisoners arrived."

On June 18, 1944, one of those prisoners would be Technician 5th Grade, John Joseph Little; however, it would not immediately be known that he was being held prisoner in Stalag 3C—for now, he was simply *missing in action*...something his wife would not be aware of for nearly a month still.

John, or Johnny as he was known to his fellow brothers in arms, had shipped out with his crew after several months of training on basic war survival skills, including shooting weapons, handling explosives and basically learning how to stay alive in combat. Given the fact that these young men were headed into a *world war*, the training seemed miniscule at best. The bulk of John's training was for Quartermaster. According to an official US Army website (http://www.quartermaster.army.mil/qm_history.h

tml), Quartermasters held a special place in the history of The United States' involvement in past wars.

"Throughout the nineteenth century the Quartermaster Department functioned differently than today's Quartermaster Corps. It did not have specialized military units. Instead Quartermasters relied upon contracted workers or detailed soldiers. The Quartermaster Department did not purchase subsistence, although it did store and transport the provisions.

All this changed in 1912, when Congress consolidated the former Subsistence, Pay, and Quartermaster Departments in order to create the Quartermaster Corps much as we know it today. It became a fully militarized organization with its own units trained to perform a host of supply and service functions on the battlefield. With this consolidation came the missions of subsistence and food service. When the Army began purchasing motorized vehicles, as early as 1903, the Quartermaster Corps assumed the new petroleum supply mission. World War I showed the increased importance of logistics in the modern era, and witnessed the first use of specialized Quartermaster units in France, including laundry, bath; salvage depots, and port operations. Quartermasters learned valuable lessons in supporting a large, modern Army overseas that would be carried into the next conflict.

During World War II, the Quartermaster Corps operated on a scale unparalleled in history, with theaters of operation in the Mediterranean, northern Europe, the Pacific, and even the China-Burma-India Theater. Thousands of soldiers were trained to fill specialized roles; and they performed heroically in far off places such as Bataan, Leyte, Salerno, Normandy, and Bastogne. At the height of the war, Quartermasters were providing over 70,000 different supply items and more than 24 million meals each day. When it was over, they had recovered and buried nearly a quarter of a million Soldiers in temporary cemeteries around the world."

John completed Quartermaster training and was then sent to England and on to France with the first wave of D-Day invaders.

On June 18, 1944, a day that started like any other day—or as "typical" as a day in the middle of a world war could be—John was riding in a Jeep that crossed paths with a German tank. Fire broke out and the jeep was overtaken by German soldiers. Once the gunfire died down, John, who was somehow now on the street, looked down and noticed that he had been shot in the leg. He had mere seconds of looking around for his fellow soldiers, before the pain of his own wound set in. It was a hot, searing pain...but he knew it wasn't life-threatening. He knew it was bad enough that he needed medical attention otherwise infection was a real threat, which could then mean losing that leg— but he wasn't overly concerned just yet. John needed to find his soldiers—the men who became brothers to him. He took one more glance at the jeep he had been riding in and his heart sank. He knew enough to know that if anyone had survived that fire, it would be a miracle; but then again, *he* was alive...so someone else had to be alive as well.

John called out for his fellow soldiers. No answer. Again, he called out. *Again...Silence.* Silence, except for the yelling coming from a foreign voice, which he would quickly realize was the German language. It was as if he was trapped in tunnel. He could hear yelling and gunfire and explosions, yet it all felt so far away and seemed muffled. Time seemed to move in slow motion. He could smell gunpowder.

He could hear the guttural screams of grown men in his periphery. It was as if everything was amplified, but muddled and confusing at the same time. His brain couldn't catch up. He blinked his eyes hard to try and make sense of everything, but that too seemed in slow motion. His eyes felt like sandpaper.

He couldn't tell if this was a dream or real life. He closed his eyes and felt his head rest on the ground. He could hear German voices growing louder, and he could feel footsteps around his body. Pretty soon he felt himself being picked up under the arms and by the legs.

His wounded leg was throbbing, and he wanted to scream, but no sound came out. His ears were ringing and his head was spinning. He was being moved into a vehicle.

"Oh shit," he thought to himself as his vision cleared a bit and he could see what was happening—he was being taken by the Germans—exactly to where, he had no idea.

John was taken by German soldiers and transported to a hospital in Berlin. He was alive—for now. The soldiers didn't say much to him, or at least anything that he could understand. They weren't particularly mean, but they weren't friendly by any stretch of the imagination either. Again, he was alive. That was about the only thing he was certain of at this point. He didn't know how many of his fellow men made it out of that ambush alive, although he figured it wasn't likely that many of them did, but he wouldn't know that for quite some time.

His life was spared, but he was in the hands of Germans—exactly where an American soldier did *not* want to find himself. At. All.

There was a bullet in his leg, his ears were ringing, his head was pounding like it was the worst hangover he ever had, and he was in a hospital. Normally, impending medical care would bring relief to anyone, but during this time in Berlin, the caliber of medical attention was scarce and subpar at best. His leg was bandaged up with something that felt more like paper than a bandage, with the bullet still inside his body; he was given a pill for the pain along with a cigarette. John was then loaded into a yet another German vehicle, crammed with other allied soldiers, many of whom were American, and driven off to God knows where. This was it.

It finally clicked what was happening. He was being taken prisoner of war. *Prisoner of War.* Aside from the banter between the German soldiers, which he still couldn't understand a word of, the ride was silent. John glanced around at the faces of the other men in captivity, and they were either completely expressionless or a shade of ghostly white with a tinge of green, stricken with a fear these men had likely never felt before.

John felt it too, in the pit of his gut. How to exactly handle being a prisoner of war was not something that was discussed extensively in training prior to deployment. The men were warned that being captured was a possibility, but beyond that, not much was said, and until faced with that as a reality, it wasn't thought about much. John had felt confident upon deployment that he understood his duties sufficiently; however, this was uncharted territory. It would be for anyone.

During the ride to the camp, John's mind drifted home. He thought of Helen. He reached for the chain around his neck, on which he wore her high school class ring. She had given it to him before they were married, and he knew that as long as he lived, he would never take it off—it would have to be pried off of his body.

John realized it would likely still be days, if not weeks, before any word got to her that he was missing or had been captured. What would she be told? Would some stranger from the War Department just tell her point blank that her husband was missing and that was it? No other information would be given to her? Would she be left to think that he was dead? Would someone be there to sit with her to answer questions and at least be a voice of comfort as she is given the information that any war wife fears and dreads from the moment their husband enlists? John knew Helen had been afraid of this very occasion from the moment he signed his papers.

Would he ever get to communicate to her that he was in fact alive—at least for now? He pictured her beautiful, striking face and her piercing blue eyes. He heard her laughter. In his mind, he could hear how she would always stir her whiskey highball drinks and clink the ice…stirring precisely three times, as if that made any difference in how the drink tasted—he always teased her about that, to which she just smiled and patted him on the shoulder, as if knowing something he did not. He thought about how she would pray at night. That woman prayed unceasingly. Helen and John both grew up Catholic, and they took their faith seriously, but there was something about Helen and her connection with a higher power, with God, that John always felt put her on a higher plane. She had such tremendous faith. He was in awe, if not in some strange way, jealous of this—at times she seemed closer to God than she did her own husband. John would think about that for a second and then realize how ridiculous he sounded.

He knew she would be praying for him and that brought him the some comfort. At this point he wasn't concerned with his own well-being at all, only Helen.

One of the captured soldiers passed John a cigarette, which he lit and took a long drag off of while contemplating the last several hours, and the rest of his life all in one long, exhausted breath.

With every bump that vehicle made, his leg throbbed and a hot, stabbing pain shot up with such a vengeance, he almost hoped he could just pass out. He was going to have to get some kind of care soon for that bullet wound. He held out a faint hope that there would be some semblance of medical care wherever it was they were being taken. He took another drag off his cigarette and closed his eyes.

Again, he could see Helen's face. He could hear her voice and see the sly grin she would give when she was telling a story that bordered on inappropriate— she was good at that. He began to feel his body relax a little for the first time in what felt like days.

He nodded off—or perhaps passed out—for a very brief moment before the shouting in German began again. The vehicle doors violently flung open and each soldier was grabbed and pulled out into the open. John blinked, got his footing and looked around. He saw buildings that resembled camps; something that you might expect to see in the wilderness and that weren't much better than being in a tent with the hard ground as a bed. Then another terrifying realization set in, almost in slow motion as he made a 365 degree turn to examine his surroundings—he had just stepped foot onto a German prison camp. The place was dark, damp and cold. The sky above was gray. "This must be what hell looks like," he thought to himself.

As far as prison camps go, John obviously had nothing to compare this to. At no point in his young life had he ever experienced something that was even remotely similar.

The bunks were nothing more than cots on a hard ground, conditions were almost as good as if they were being kept in horse stables, and the smell probably wasn't much better. The Red Cross was finally able to get supplies, such as food, toiletries, and other basic necessities, to the captured soldiers, but those were immediately confiscated by the Germans. Each week those Red Cross bags would arrive…and each week the captured soldiers would sign for their bags only to have them taken. The Germans would taunt the prisoners, pulling the items out, making sure each one could be seen, sought after, and then snatched away. One German guard in particular made John's skin crawl. He made eye contact with John as he was going through his Red Cross delivery, looked at him with the evil grin of a Cheshire cat, and muttered something inaudible under his breath while walking away with the goods that were sent for John. This went on as long as the Red Cross sent supplies. Because of this, many of the prisoners' teeth began to rot. They weren't getting proper hygiene supplies, which included toothpaste and a toothbrush. They were able to sneak cigarettes here and there, which didn't help the dental hygiene situation at all. They were not fed proper nutrition for meals, so their bodies, which were once strong and in prime physical condition, began to deteriorate into poorer health by the day. There was some sort of a camp physician who would pour antiseptic into John's bullet wound in his leg to keep it from getting infected & then put a new bandage around it every other day or so; but that's as far as medical treatment for being shot went.

As far as whether or not any physical abuse from the Germans took place, one can only guess. There are numerous articles and accounts of the violent & inhumane conditions the prisoners had to endure in these camps, including Stalag 3C.

July 10, 1944 was a Monday. Helen didn't sleep well the night before and woke up tired, agitated and anxious. She didn't recall any particular dreams, so she couldn't figure out what her problem was. The sun was shining, and the sky was blue; the typical Missouri-in-July humidity hung thick on the air—nothing was out of the ordinary she thought. She made her way to the bathroom to splash water on her face and to try and shake off the feeling of dread that was hanging over her.

She slipped on her bathrobe and went to the kitchen to make coffee. She decided to avoid the newspaper this particular morning—she figured any bad news would just worsen the anxiety she already felt. She got dressed and began getting ready for work, when there was a knock at the door.

Helen felt herself shudder as a shot of adrenaline pulsed through her and caused her body to shake. She surprised herself at just how jumpy she was.

She had to tell herself to get it together; it was probably her neighbor, Beth, coming over to gossip about the latest smut article she read in some trashy magazine or wanting to gossip about the new neighbors down the street.

She slowly went to the door and as she turned the doorknob, she could see through the frosted glass window that it was very clearly not Beth—it was a man. He was wearing a uniform. Once she opened the door, and could see him clearly, her heart nearly stopped. Time stopped. Everything the uniformed man did and said was in complete slow motion, and hazy. He took off his hat and placed it under his arm.

He slowly looked up and met her eyes with his own—they were blank. There was no emotion whatsoever.

"Are you Mrs. John Little?" ,the officer asked.

"Ye-..." Helen had to clear her throat since no sound was coming out..."Yes, I am," she said in a hushed, hesitant whisper.

"Ma'am, I'm here on behalf of the War Department of the United States, I have a telegram for you from the Adjutant General's office in Washington D.C., May I come in?" Helen didn't even answer him. She wanted to scream "No, you cannot come in and tell me that my husband is dead or injured so badly he will soon be dead! GO AWAY!" Of course she didn't say a word, she just barely moved out of the way and opened the door a bit further so that he could enter. She motioned for him to have a seat, but he declined.

"Mrs. Little, I regret to inform you that your husband has been declared missing in action since June 18th in France. I'm very sorry. That is all the information I have at this time, another letter will come from the War Department with further details."

And with that, he handed Helen the telegram, put his hat on and wished her the best, and as easily as he had walked into her home and shattered her heart in a matter of seconds, he was gone. She didn't even know his name.

Helen stood in the doorway and watched him drive off. She stood there for a few moments that felt like an eternity—just staring off into space. The sky was still blue. The sun was still shining. The birds were still singing. People were still going to work. Children were likely going to find some way to stay cool on this 100+ degree day. Yet her world had just stopped. Helen had been growing increasingly anxious over the fact that she hadn't heard from John in a few weeks, but that wasn't entirely out of the ordinary—letters took weeks to arrive. If she had thought too long about it, it would've bothered her, but she hadn't allowed herself to give it too much thought and still figured no news was good news.

Well, here was her news. In the form of a thin piece of paper with two sentences that could very well alter the course of her and John's life that they had planned together.

Helen backed away from the door, closed it and stepped back into her living room. Her sister, Arlene, had already gone to work. She was all alone now. She sat down on the sofa and picked up a handmade blanket that her mother had crocheted for her a few years before when she moved to Kirksville to begin her one year of college. She picked it up and allowed her fingers to examine the stitching; she slowly pulled that blanket up to her face and allowed the tears to come. A violent cry came out of the depths of Helen's body and was muffled by the blanket.

Tears poured out of her eyes like water running out of a faucet. It felt hot coming down her cheeks. Her temples started to throb with every breath she took, which lead to an even harder, louder cry. She lay down and cradled that blanket close to her chest. Missing in action. *Missing in action.* What did that even mean? She hoped that it meant that he was still alive—for now. John could be dead and they just haven't found him yet. This could be the War

Department's way of buying some time before delivering even worse news to her. Every awful scenario crossed Helen's mind. John being dead was obviously the worst. But the fact that he could be captured by the enemy, having to endure torture, not being fed, being terrified and alone—on the other side of the world—that thought was almost too much for Helen to bear right now.

The thoughts swirling through her mind made her feel sick. She thought about calling in sick to work—if she told them what she had just found out, they would understand. But then she would be left sitting alone in her apartment all day, crumpled up in a ball on her couch sobbing until Arlene came home and found her—that didn't seem like the best option either.

Helen took a deep breath, folded her blanket back up just as it was, went to the bathroom to fix her hair and touch up her face, and she smoothed her clothes and stepped outside and went to work.

The remarkable thing about Helen is that she has an uncanny ability to compartmentalize situations. When she was at work, she was at work. She focused on her job.

She was one of the lucky ladies of that era to have a great office job and she intended to keep it. After all, she wasn't the only war wife having to navigate this terrible, uncertain news. Her day went by in a blur. She got home, and Arlene was waiting for her at the door. She was holding the telegram that Helen had left on the coffee table. Helen all but collapsed into Arlene's arms, and they both cried. Arlene made Helen some dinner, and they sat at the kitchen table to talk. They cried and talked, and they prayed. Helen didn't feel particularly prepared for this journey, however long it may be and however it may end, yet here she was.

She was in this now and she took a vow to be with John in good times and in bad and she meant it—

and she would lean on that vow every second of every day going forward during this time.

Arlene finally convinced Helen to go to bed around midnight. She was dreading the nighttime. She didn't want to lie in bed thinking of John. He wasn't just "overseas in a war," now he was "missing in action" and very likely fighting for his life, assuming he was even still alive. She had to catch herself when she thought like that. He *was still alive*, she would remind herself. She couldn't give up on him—she wouldn't—ever. She would spend the next few hours of the night fighting that painful, choking lump in her throat; if she entertained it, the tears would come, and she wasn't sure they would stop.

She swallowed hard, took a deep breath, rolled to her side, prayed to God to protect John and then finally fell asleep.

After what seemed like only minutes, Helen blinked her eyes to see the sun coming through her window.

She smelled coffee so she knew Arlene was still home. She made her way down the hallway to the kitchen. She could feel the dried tear streaks on her cheeks, her eyes burned and her head was pounding. Arlene had a concerned look on her face as she handed Helen a cup of coffee.

"What's wrong now?" Helen asked.

"I wanted to stay home with you while you saw this, then I have to go to work…I can call in though if you need me to. Turn to page 5A." Arlene handed Helen the St. Louis Post Dispatch newspaper for Tuesday July 11, 1944.

Helen opened the paper and saw the headline: "Six Killed in Action from St. Louis Area," and she looked to the right and the fourth photo in a row of sixteen photos was her beloved John. There was that sweet little hint of a smile she had been missing. The caption above the photos read 'Casualties from this Area.'

Helen dropped her coffee and the mug shattered into several sharp pieces and startled Arlene.

"WHAT?! CASUALTY?! HE'S....DEAD? They said *MISSING IN ACTION!*" Helen could feel her heart beginning to pound out of her chest, and panic began to rise up through her body and into her throat in the form of a flash so hot she thought she might choke on her own breath. Arlene grabbed her arm to calm her, and she told her to read the rest of the article.

Each soldier had a blurb about them and their whereabouts or condition, so Helen quickly scanned down to the sixth man from the bottom's blurb, which read:

"Cpl. John Joseph Little, 26, a member of the Quartermaster Corps, has been missing in action since June 18 in France. His wife, Mrs. Helen Little, lives at 5838 Enright Avenue."

"That's *it?*" Helen thought. She caught her breath and composed herself. She hadn't even noticed that Arlene was sweeping up the broken glass from around her bare feet. Why had the newspaper lumped John in with casualties? Did that mean they knew something she didn't? She shook her head and stopped that thought in its tracks.

She figured it would only be a matter of time now before the neighbors started coming by to check up on her—she fully expected her nosy neighbor Beth to start coming over with various forms of casseroles or anything else that could be frozen and re-heated, wanting to "be a friendly shoulder to cry on," but all the while really just wanting the latest news to chat to the other neighborhood women about. Her coworkers would undoubtedly know by now, and Arlene had already told their siblings and parents. Helen had a good support system, of which she was very thankful for. This could be a long journey; one that she prayed would have a happy ending. It was very hard to keep the faith with the number of casualties in the newspapers being shown and discussed much more frequently than happy endings.

Helen glanced back over that article one more time, scanning the photos of these young men—boys really. The photos were their official military photos—yet oddly enough they were all smiling. They looked so confident, so happy, so...*alive*. But some were the faces of a woman's fiancé or husband, a child's father, a mother's son, someone's brother, someone's friend. Some of these faces were of men who would not be coming home—ever again. These were men from St. Louis. While none of the names rang an immediate bell for Helen, she thought it was very possible that she could've known them or their families at some point. She ripped that tiny photo of John out of the article and put it in her pocketbook. She clung to the hope that he would not end up actually being a casualty in the next newspaper article.

Once Helen got her wits about her again, she did what she did every day. She got dressed and drove herself to work.

Day after day in the immediate weeks following the news that John was missing in action, letters would arrive from various family members, past co-workers, friends from Camp Tyson, etc. John's most recent company that he was employed with, Rice-Stix, was particularly kind and thoughtful during this ordeal. Immediately upon seeing the news in the St. Louis Post-Dispatch, a letter from John Ayres with Rice-Stix was delivered and read:

July 12, 1944

Dear Mrs. Little,

The morning paper lists John as missing in action in France. We, at the Factory, who worked with John, are so sorry to hear this, but hope that word of him will soon be forthcoming. No doubt, the message that you have received has brought you some sorrow, but with the action taking place so fast over there, please do not give up hope that he is alright. Many of our boys are reported missing, then word is heard from them at a later date.......again, expressing our hopes to you that he is alright and you will

soon hear from him.

We remain,

Yours Very Truly,

RICE-STIX TRUNK FACTORY

John A. Ayres

Another letter from the War Department arrived that was a follow up to the very brief and impersonal telegram delivery from a few days prior.

July 14, 1944

Dear Mrs. Little:

This letter is to confirm my recent telegram in which you were regretfully informed that your husband, Technician Fifth Grade John J. Little, 37,401,569, Quartermaster Corps, has been reported missing in action since June 18, 1944 in France.

I know that added distress is caused by failure to receive more information or details. Therefore, I wish to assure you that at any time additional information is received, it will be transmitted to you without delay, and if in the meantime no additional information is received, I will again communicate with you at the expiration of three months.

The term "missing in action" is used only to indicate that the whereabouts or status of an individual is not immediately known. It is not intended to convey the impression that the case is closed. I wish to emphasize that every effort is exerted continuously to clear up the status of our personnel. Under war conditions this is a difficult task as you must readily realize. Experience has shown that many persons reported missing in action are subsequently reported as prisoners of war, but as this information is furnished by countries with which we are at war, the War Department is helpless to expedite such reports. However, in order to relieve financial worry, Congress has enacted legislation which continues in force

the pay, allowances and allotments to dependents of
personnel being carried in a missing status.
Permit me to extend to you my heartfelt sympathy during
this period of uncertainty.

Sincerely yours,
J.A.ULIO
Major General
The Adjutant General

Over the next several weeks various letters of the same sentiment came from the US Senate and other government branches. Helen knew these were merely formalities and that likely only one original copy was ever thoughtfully typed up—these were simply tailored repeats at this point, being sent out in bulk to a nation of grieving and worried people. The thought kept crossing her mind that their fourth wedding anniversary had also come and gone on July 19th. Only four years.

Helen felt like she and John had already lived a lifetime together—yet four years was hardly any time at all. There was so much life ahead for the two of them, and she prayed he would make it back to be with her for it.

The letters piled up on her coffee table, and she carried on with her normal life as much as she could—or at least tried to adjust to her *new normal* which meant holding her chin up, getting her job done and getting accustomed to a state of being constantly worried. Butterflies in her stomach were a normal feeling now. Days dragged on, she kept up her job at the medical book company, she kept up with friends and managed to lead a very seemingly normal existence—with one huge piece missing; the man that forever held a piece of her heart.

August 16, 1944 was a Wednesday. A little more than a month had passed knowing that John was unaccounted for; not knowing if he was alive or dead. A little more than two months had gone by since the date the War Department said he went missing. A knock came to Helen's door once again as she was preparing to leave that morning for work and immediately the flush of panic began to rise up into her throat and her head started to feel light and dizzy. She inched up to the door and cracked it open enough to see a man standing there.

He wasn't in a military uniform so she allowed herself to breathe and she opened the door. He identified himself as a representative from Western Union and he handed her a small piece of paper which read in all capital block letters:

"REPORT JUST RECEIVED THROUGH THE INTERNATIONAL RED CROSS STATES THAT YOUR HUSBAND TECHNICIAN FIFTH

GRADE JOHN J LITTLE IS A PRISONER OF
WAR OF THE GERMAN GOVERNMENT.
LETTER OF INFORMATION FOLLOWS
FROM PROVOST MARSHAL GENERAL=ULIO
THE ADJUTANT GENERAL."

Helen had to blink hard several times to see the words correctly through the tears she hadn't realized were clouding up her eyes and would inevitably be streaming down her cheeks. Was she reading this correctly?

This means John is alive! She couldn't even jump up and down or scream with delight or make any noise at all for that matter. She let out a long, drawn out exhale, sat down on the couch and closed her eyes. "Thank you God," she softly said. "Thank you."

She scanned over the words once more.

He was now prisoner of war—in a German camp. Now a whole new wave of terror flooded her. She knew that wasn't a good thing. Sure, he was alive, but in what condition? The news played out horror stories of the Germans—how they hated Americans and the terror they inflicted upon the prisoners they held. Helen didn't know what was true and what was being sensationalized by the media. John was alive, but for how long?

A different kind of fear settled into the marrow of Helen's being; a fear that would put a very tight grip on her for months still.

Fall came and went in St. Louis. The war was still the main topic of conversation at work, church and in the newspapers. Lives were being lost every single day. Helen wasn't sure if progress was being made or not. The holidays came and went, and the harsh St. Louis winter set in for the next few months. Helen's sisters and family were her rocks during this time. Her job also acted as somewhat of a saving grace.

She had something to channel her thoughts and energy on during the day, at least until she went home. Arlene was always good for some comic relief when times were tough.

She could make Helen laugh no matter how hard Helen tried not to. Arlene and Helen both had a wicked sense of humor, and that would often help them lighten up any situation. Once the two of them got to giggling with each other, it was hard to get them to stop. The old saying goes that "laughter is the best medicine," and Helen found that to be very true. The two would make a fire in the fireplace, get warm on their couch and sip their whiskey highball drinks while talking about childhood stories, reminiscing about people they knew growing up or in high school and wondering what happened to some of them. Inevitably, Artie Langanecker was always a topic for comedic fodder. The girls would remember that red-headed boy and the crush he had on Helen for their entire time in school.

That boy, bless his heart, tried every trick in the book to get Helen to go on a date with him, and nothing worked. They often joked about where he might have ended up in life, for neither of them had heard anything about ol' Artie since they graduated high school. These stories took Helen's mind off John for a just tiny bit, but he was never far from her thoughts.

In late winter 1945, Helen received word of John's location, and she was permitted to send him letters and parcels addressed to United States Prisoner of War number: 81927, Stalag 3C, Germany. Winter dragged on in St. Louis, but Helen had renewed hope now that she could communicate with John even just a little bit. Just the fact that he had an address now provided the tiniest feeling of relief. She didn't like the fact that he was now reduced to an ID number rather than a human being—she prayed he wasn't being treated like just another number as well. As news of John's situation made the rounds in Helen's family, work and church, she felt a great sense of community surrounding her. Her church family prayed every Sunday for John's safe return, as well as the safe return of all of the soldiers and for an end to the war—there was never a shortage of food in her apartment thanks to kind and often overly-concerned, but well-meaning neighbors. This was especially a blessing since neither Helen nor Arlene were a fan of cooking. Those two could throw back some whiskey, but when it came to cooking, they'd just as soon have someone else do it.

The winter was beginning to thaw out in St. Louis by March, and there were very slight signs of spring on the horizon. Trees had begun to sprout tiny green buds that would eventually give way to lush summer leaves. The chill in the air began to disappear during the day, long enough to provide enough warmth to sit outside and get some sunshine. Helen found herself beginning to sleep a little better and overall somehow feel more at ease. Maybe it was the season changing and the promise of something new on the horizon. Or maybe it was just the fact that with winter gone, she no longer had to face dreary days and cold nights fearing for John. The sun helped her mood and that raised her spirits.

March 15, 1945 brought another familiar knock to the door.

It wasn't the dainty knock of one of the neighbor ladies; it was the hard formal knock of a man. A stranger.

It was the knock that Helen had come to dread with every fiber of her being—the very knock that sent a chill down her spine and would almost render her paralyzed for a split second before going to the door. Is this going to be the day that she got the news she feared more than anything? Is this going to be the day that she hears "we regret to inform you…" followed by "please accept our deepest sympathy during this time"…followed by being handed a pamphlet that offered advice and counseling to war widows along with funeral planning help?

All of those thoughts raced through her head in a matter of seconds as she slowly and cautiously walked to the front door and felt her adrenaline shoot through her veins once again as she discovered through the frosted glass that the person on the other side was indeed a uniformed man. She cracked the door and could make out enough to see that he was not in a military uniform, but again a representative from Western Union. Helen relaxed a little. He handed her a telegram. She thanked him politely and shut the door. This time she took a deep breath and sat on the couch to compose herself before opening the letter to read the following, again in all capital dark block letters:

"I AM PLEASED TO INFORM YOU REPORT RECEIVED FROM UNITED STATES MILITARY MISSION IN MOSCOW STATES YOUR HUSBAND TECHNICIAN FIFTH GRADE JOHN J LITTLE PREVIOUSLY REPORTED A PRISONER OF WAR HAS BEEN RELEASED FROM A GERMAN PRISONER OF WAR CAMP AND IS NOW PRESUMED TO BE IN POLAND. THE WAR DEPARTMENT INVITES SUBMISSION OF A MESSAGE NOT TO EXCEED TWENTY FIVE WORDS FOR ATTEMPTED DELIVERY TO HIM. MESSAGE SHOULD BE ADDRESSED TO CASUALTY

BRANCH, A-G-O ROOM TWENTY FIVE
FIFTEEN. MUNITIONS BUILDING. FURTHER
INFORMATION WILL BE FURNISHED WHEN
RECEIVED."
J.A. ULIO
THE ADJUTANT GENERAL

This time Helen let out a happy cry; the kind of reaction that is half-crying, half-laughing. Her heart was flooded with an emotion she hadn't felt in a very long time, pure happiness. He was one step closer to being home. She wasn't sure how John got to Poland, nor did she have any idea of the circumstances he was facing there, but she had to believe with all she had that it was a better situation than being in a German POW camp. Arlene was coming in just as Helen was folding up the letter and making note of the address she could send a letter to John to.

Arlene wasn't used to seeing Helen so giddy for the past several months so a look of bewilderment spread over her face upon walking into the living room to see Helen.

"Wow, what is it? You obviously just got good news", Arlene said.

"He's free...John's FREE! Well, he's in Poland, and I have no idea what that means just yet, but he's free from the German prison camp! He's alive, and he's out of the hands of Germans!" Helen all but squealed as Arlene hugged her tight, and they decided this called for a drink. They sat on the porch together and filled in some of the neighbors who passed by and enjoyed the evening outside until the early spring air turned chilly again, and they retired inside for the night.

That was the first night in so many long months Helen had truly had a peaceful night's sleep.

She said prayers of thanks to God, over and over.

She let her body and her mind relax, and exhaustion from the last several months took over, and she fell into the deepest sleep she had had in what felt like forever.

Helen would later learn that John's camp had been liberated by the Russians and communication was very fuzzy during that time period at best. An article in the St. Louis Post-Dispatch on March 17, 1945 tells of "approximately 1200 former war prisoners freed from German hands by the Russian advance, arrived at a Middle East Port and are now enroute to the United States." It would seem that John spent very little time in Poland, and that was simply a cross point to get to Cairo and then on to the United States.

The article goes on to say that "the liberated men appeared to be in good physical condition, despite hardships and dangers they had but recently survived while escaping from the Nazi guards or prison pens to make their way in the midst of battle to the Russian lines. They were outfitted in the patchwork remains of Allied uniforms, including items of Soviet Army issue."

Letters were coming to Helen's apartment in frenzy, many of which had overlapping dates. Helen had a hard time making sense of it, until one letter from the local war office stood out. John would be returning home. Helen received word that his ship had come in and he, along with 69 other repatriated American soldiers would be arriving at Jefferson Barracks in St. Louis on April 8, 1945.

Helen's entire world changed…again…for the very best this time. The nightmare was over. He was coming back to her and in one piece. She realized just how lucky she was. April 8th couldn't come fast enough. Helen and Arlene spent an absurd amount of time trying to figure out what she should wear to meet John. Once she had the perfect outfit picked out, Arlene helped her do her hair just right and her make-up was just right—everything was coming together. Helen got in the car and began the short drive to Jefferson Barracks. With every turn she could feel the butterflies taking flight in her stomach again, much like she felt on the day John introduced himself to her on those church steps years ago. She realized that she was holding her breath and the thought of that made her laugh and think about how ridiculous that was. This was her *husband*, not some stranger. The last several months had been such a rollercoaster though, and she was slightly nervous at the state he might be in. How would he look? Would he be thin? Would he even look remotely the same? Would he be disturbed by what he had been through? Was it as horrible as the stories she made up in her mind and as awful as the news made everything sound?

She pulled into Jefferson Barracks, and there was already quite a crowd growing. Women and children and mothers and fathers, all anxiously awaiting the arrival of the boys they sent off, returning now as men—happy to be returning at all. Helen made her way into the crowd, and since she was alone, it was easy to squeeze into a spot in the front.

Soon a bus came around the side of the main building, and the crowd erupted. The attendees had all been given a little American flag, and everyone was waving them proudly to welcome their soldiers home, including Helen. She began to feel the excitement well up in her, she could hardly stand it! One by one the soldiers stepped off the bus. For the most part, they looked in decent condition Helen thought, maybe a little thin, but overall, considering what they had been through, they seemed ok. Then she saw him. She'd recognize that smile from a mile away. She must've pushed a few people out of the way, but Helen made a mad dash for John, to hell with the rules that said you had to stay behind a barricade—she was going to her man!

She jumped into his arms and he picked her up, spun her around and planted the biggest kiss on her that he possibly could; a kiss in which a photographer from the St. Louis Post would capture and the caption would read *"Together Again."* There was no better caption for that moment. It was perfect. All was right with the world. Helen noticed John had a pretty significant limp that he brushed off as "nothing big," when in fact it would be the bullet that remained lodged in his leg. His teeth looked like they needed some care, but other than that, he was as handsome as ever and looked healthy enough considering the circumstances. They hurried to the car and she got in, got settled behind the wheel and before putting the keys in the ignition she stopped and looked over at John. She had to check one more time to be sure this was real—that he was actually sitting in the car next to her, in the flesh. He actually was home, and this nightmare was over, and they were free to live the life they'd imagined. She didn't even have to say a word as his eyes met hers and he gave her that grin that she fell in love with—the grin that years before solidified the knowledge in her heart that John Joseph Little was the man she was going to marry, the grin that she saw in her dreams all the nights she tried to sleep without him by her side. That grin was as real as the man sitting next to her. She didn't know anything about his experience, and she wouldn't know much ever, but right now none of that mattered. He was here. They were together—and together they drove to a St. Louis hotel where they could spend their first night together in several months, completely alone—with only each other. John would slowly acclimate to civilian life again. He would have his leg wound properly treated, and his teeth would be fixed. He would put a few pounds on due to proper nutrition again, but the one piece Helen couldn't "fix" would be the awful memories in his mind that would take up residency there for the rest of his life.

"In all the world, there is no heart for me like yours. In all the world, there is no love for you like mine." — *Maya Angelou*

Photos from days gone by

Helen & her sisters, circa early 1940s. From left to right: Betty, Gracie, Jimmy, Arlene, Helen & Geraldine (later known as Sister Miriam Joseph, after entering the convent)

A young John Little looking
dapper after entering the United
States Armed Forces

John & Helen at the
beginning of their marriage

July 19, 1941. Helen & John's
wedding day.

John & Helen at Camp McCoy in
Wisconsin

Young & in love

"Together Again." photo captured by a photographer for the St. Louis Post-Dispatch at John's homecoming on April 8, 1945

John with five of his six children
in August of 1957 in front of their
Cape Girardeau, Missouri home.

John & Helen with their six children on
oldest son Joe's wedding day. From left to
right: Ann, Mary, Susan, Tom, Dan, Helen,
John & Joe

Helen's graduation from Southeast
Missouri State University with her
Master's Degree in Education in
1974

A snapshot of a love that would
endure forever. Helen & John in
the late 1970s

Helen blinked again. This time she had to blink away tears. She wasn't a crier; not since she had to live through John's captivity. She always told herself that nothing would be as tough to get through as that and that thought alone kept her from being an overly emotional person. So, the fact that she was about to lose her cool in front of her children and anyone else that might be in sight of her was just unnecessary to her. An entire lifetime had just flashed before her eyes. In reality, only about 30 minutes had passed in that musty auditorium on the campus of Southeast Missouri State University, but in her mind's eye, it had been more than 40 years.

She saw her entire life. The good, the bad, the scary, the beautiful.....she realized her own miracle. Her sweet husband had come back. He was her wild card. And what a blessed wild card he was.

God had known the future she was meant to have with him. He protected her and the life that was meant to be, and he brought her beloved John back to her safe and sound and in one piece. Helen has always acknowledged the fact that while agonizing and feeling like an eternity as it was happening, John's time in captivity was relatively short compared to some soldiers who spent a year or more being held prisoner of war.

The immediate time that followed John's return home is a bit of a mystery—as is the entire time he spent in Stalag 3C. The knowledge of John's personal experience stops at the very basic information of lack of hygiene and no nutrition, the fact that his supplies from the Red Cross were confiscated on a weekly basis and the Russians—who liberated the prisoners—stole almost everything that the Germans did not, including Helen's class ring that John always kept with him on a chain around his neck. The rest of his experience with the German soldiers holding him captive would stay locked away in his mind until the day he died. He did not speak of it, nor write of it. There is one piece of evidence that gives a bit of a glimpse into his world as a prisoner—on the back of a wooden cigarette case, John had scribbled a drawing of himself in his army uniform behind a barbed wire fence, with a drawing of the buildings that resembles what the prison camps actually did look like. On the other side of the case in scribbled writing is some semblance of a timeline of his captivity. Even when his oldest son Joe entered the National Guard, John wouldn't speak of this part of his life.

His family sensed that much worse took place than he would ever let on and unfortunately that would remain in his mind, left to torture him silently for the rest of his days.

John's oldest daughter Susan remembers that when the American prisoners were released from captivity during Vietnam and their rescue was shown on the evening news on television, she glanced over at her father who sat quietly in his chair as tears streamed down his cheeks. He knew what they had been through. He felt it in his heart as he watched their release—it was almost as if he finally had a connection to someone who had been through the exact same horror he had been through years before. What the exact details of that horror were, we will never know.

Eventually John would get a good job with the 7-Up Bottling Company, and he would move Helen and their young family to Cape Girardeau, Missouri, just about two hours south of St. Louis. There they would raise their six children: Joe, Dan, Tom, Susan, Mary and Ann.

Helen would have the chance to be the mother she envisioned being the moment she first laid eyes on John Joseph Little that beautiful fall day in Millwood, Missouri. Helen's children were her pride and joy. She was a strong and stern, but compassionate and loving mother. Her kids didn't get away with much, but they were raised to respect everyone, try their best in school and were encouraged to follow their dreams, whatever they may be.

As Helen's children grew older and the youngest, Ann, was in grade school, the deep-lurking urge to go back into teaching began creeping up more and more—so much so that Helen could not ignore it anymore. Up until this time, after having children, Helen was still working part-time as a secretary for various companies. She still wasn't one to sit around at all and having six mouths to feed didn't make staying at home a possibility. But she couldn't ignore this feeling.

It was blaring so hard in her mind and in her heart—she NEEDED to go back to school to finish her education to become a teacher.

After talking with John, they both agreed she would go back to college. A dream that she did not even think was a possibility the first time around in 1940, was still a dream, except now it was at her fingertips.

Prior to the early 1970s, Southeast Missouri State University was still called Southeast Missouri Teacher's College. Helen would enroll as a sophomore undergraduate, since she had completed one year of college so many years before. In between packing lunches, helping her children with homework, being a wife and maintaining a home, and working a part time job, Helen would study. She would disappear into her textbooks and soak up as much as she possibly could. Her oldest daughter Susan recalls a time when her grade school biology class required her to collect bugs to study and report on; her mother was also in a college biology class—which also required her to collect bugs.

So off Helen and her daughter went to collect their bugs and work on their respective reports together. While Susan was focusing hard on gathering the bugs she needed, carefully checking each one off a list given to her by the teacher, Helen stopped for a moment—she glanced up at Susan, her long blonde hair almost glowing in the late afternoon sunshine. "This is a moment," she thought. Something that— although tiny and seemingly insignificant—was magic. She closed her eyes for a split second to commit it to memory. She looked up and said a silent "thank you" to God for the blessings in her life; the blessing that *IS her life*. Perhaps if she hadn't been through almost losing John, she wouldn't appreciate these tiny blink-and-you-miss-it moments.

God protected her and guided her then, and He was guiding this new journey through college for her now. The fact that she could be her peers' mother made no difference to her whatsoever. She studied hard and made excellent grades. She was sure, now more than ever before that education was her calling. Cape Girardeau had an excellent public school system, and she could not wait to be a part of it. She would go on to complete her student teaching at Alma Schrader Elementary School, and on April 22, 1968, she would receive a typed job offer from the school to begin on August 26th. For her very first teaching contract, she would earn $578.94 per month. Upon signing her contract, it was not yet known what grade she would be assigned to, however she soon found out she would be teaching the sixth grade, which is where she would remain until she retired.

Helen would then go on to earn her Master's Degree and complete several more hours of training and education—anything she could do to ensure a good retirement for herself and her family, since she was considerably late getting into the game as a teacher. Her students would remember her as a very good teacher—creative, innovative, stern, but caring. Even now, all these years later since her retirement in 1988, her former students remember her fondly. Since she was quite a bit older than the other new teachers, not much shenanigans got past her, and kids didn't attempt to test her too much.

Helen and John's children would all grow up to have successful lives and careers of their own.

By the late 1960s, she was already a grandmother and would go on to have many more grandchildren. All of her grandchildren would hold her on sort of a mystical pedestal. She would always infuse education in with fun time at her house. One of the favorite activities she would participate in with her grandkids was BINGO. It sounds simple enough….but when you played BINGO with Helen Little, you played for money. Yes, us young kids played BINGO for payment…but there was a catch: You played with various coins and if you yelled "BINGO!", you had to count your money for her, count it *correctly* and then you could stash it away in your pocket and dream of what little trinket you were going to buy when you won a few more games and got a little richer…or until you had enough to at least earn bragging rights among the other kids. That very activity is how most of us kids learned how to count money for the first time.

Growing up as one of Helen's grandchildren, a love of reading was also instilled at an early age. She would keep baskets of books within reach of little hands and would drop whatever she was doing to sit and read a book, but what would end up happening is the child would end up reading the book out loud with her guidance, her patience. *The Three Billy Goats Gruff* and *I'll Love You Forever, I'll Like You for Always* were two of the favorites in her house. One of her grandsons, Brian, has vivid memories of sitting at the kitchen table with her and John, who was affectionately called Pepaw. At that time, the living room television set was on a cart with wheels.

She would spin that cart right around from the living room, into the archway of the kitchen and as dinner was being served, and one could often find Hee-Haw on TV.

Perhaps some of my own most vivid memories are playing in her basement. Back then it seemed so much bigger, a touch on the scary side due to the copious amounts of crickets that had taken up residency down there, but always somewhat magical. Hideous and loud orange carpet lined the hardwood steps and unfinished floor—and still does to this day—and offered some semblance of padding on an otherwise cold, concrete floor.

The texture of the carpet more resembled that of a Brillo pad than soft carpeting. The lights were turned on by a long string hanging from a single lightbulb on the unfinished ceiling. There was a couch on one side of the staircase and a bed on the other—this made for great (and dangerous) adventures of seeing how high we could go up on the steps and still be brave enough to jump on the mattress and couch cushions set up below. There were several bookshelves that were always good for finding a book to transport you back in time the minute it was opened.

But the jewel of the basement was the toy barrel. Yes, an actual *BARREL*. I am one of only three granddaughters. Our oldest cousin Barb grew up in Ohio and wasn't around except for special occasions.

My cousin Danielle and I are exactly one year and two days apart in age. We grew up together. Memaw's house was our haven. We had "girls nights," where no boys were allowed. We would spend HOURS upon HOURS in that basement…digging in that barrel of "treasures." To our young minds, that barrel was the entrance into a new world. Memaw's wedding dress was in that barrel along with an old graduation gown and some fun shoes from the 1940s, just to name a few items. Items that now, looking back, were probably being eaten by moths and crickets at the bottom of that barrel—but to us, they were absolute treasures that would allow us to dream the minute we put them on. We would play "house" in that basement for hours.

Or we would sit and go through old books or old items on the shelves and wonder what they were from, what they meant. We were wise enough back then to know we had something special. We had *someone* special. And thankfully, as I write this, we still do.

John's health would be on the decline as he got older. He had lung issues from smoking and congestive heart failure. It would also be discovered that he had a benign brain tumor which caused many residual health problems. John would suffer a stroke in his later years that would leave him unable to speak properly or be independent at all. He would be only a shell of the man he once was. He was only in his late 60s—the same age my own father is now as I type this.

As a child in the early 1980s, I regret that my only memories are of him sitting in his chair staring blankly at the world going on around him. I wonder now if he was in there somewhere. Did he know how many grandkids he had? Did he hear us running around, giggling and causing a loud ruckus, especially on our annual Christmas Eve night? I did not get to share stories with him. I did not get to know him…most of his grandchildren, in fact, would miss out on knowing this great man in person.

John Joseph Little passed away on September 25, 1985. He was only 67 years old, but due to all of his health problems, he looked so much older. I look at photos now and think he looked about 80 when in fact he wasn't that old at all. He would be Helen's only love. She knew that his final years were not the way anyone would wish to live, and he wasn't the same John she knew so many years before, but Helen loved that man something fierce until his very last breath on this earth. And she missed him with every fiber of her being. Even though it had been quite some time since he had spoken a full sentence or eaten a meal without her help or even took a step without her help, she could close her eyes and still hear his laugh and see his smile. Those beautiful, kind eyes would forever be burned in her memory, and she was so thankful for that.

While the house was often filled with Helen's grown children and grandchildren on a daily basis—someone was always coming and going—the nighttime always came again. She would lie in bed, again, keeping his side open just as she had done so many years before when she didn't know if he was coming home at all, only this time she knew he wasn't coming back. The love of her life was in Heaven now—she did take comfort in that. He had lived one amazing life, even though somewhat short it seemed, and she got to be part of it. He could've died in that prison camp, but instead he was given about 40 additional years to create a wonderful life with Helen and their children. In some ways he was just an ordinary Missouri boy who went off to war, was captured, released, came home, raised a family and worked hard to make an honest living and provide for his family.

But to Helen, he was her everything, and he was extraordinary. He was the man God had picked out for her. He was the father to their six children. He was the man that encouraged her to follow her dreams even when that meant that things would be tight at home money-wise, and it was fairly uncommon for a mother of six to decide to go back to school and put her own ambitions for a career as a high priority. During that time, most men would not have been as supportive. Then again, John Joseph Little was no ordinary man. He was her hero. He was her best friend. And now, while relatively still young, in her 60s, she was going to have to figure out what life without her beloved John by her side looked like. It was only in the silence of the night that she let her mind wander again to that feeling of sadness and uncertainty in the pit of her stomach. True, things were very different now than they were back when he was captured and their future was unknown.

There were no six children, no house full of grandchildren. Now Helen had many friends and family to call on and to keep company with. But in the quiet of the night, alone in the bed they used to share, she felt just as alone now as she did more than 40 years before. She would talk to John, she would pray for him. And even through tears she trusted that she would indeed see him again one day. Who knows when that day will come, but when it does, she knows it will be like seeing him that day he stepped off that bus at Jefferson Barracks all over again. And with that thought in her mind and in her heart, she would fall asleep. The sun always came up the next day, and she had a busy life to lead.

Helen would retire from teaching in the spring of 1988. Once again, not being the type to sit around and twiddle her thumbs with all of her free time she would become busier and lead even more of a full, vibrant life than she even imagined possible.

She became extremely active in her church, St. Vincent de Paul Catholic Church. She would volunteer for many organizations within the church and within the community of Cape Girardeau, giving back and serving wherever and whenever she could.

It was also during her retirement that she would discover a love of traveling. She would go on to visit all fifty states with her friends and her favorite part of traveling would be taking 'mystery trips' where the travelers were not told where they would be going until they were at or near their destination. She thrived on seeing the country and several parts of the world, including Egypt and the Holy Lands. Sometimes during quiet moments on long flights or tedious bus rides her mind would drift back to her days in Millwood, Missouri.

Who could've possibly known back then, that a little girl from the most dirt poor family in town would one day realize all of her dreams—she would get to be a teacher, she would marry the man of her dreams, she would get to raise a family, she would get to travel and see the world. Helen would get lost in daydreaming occasionally during those moments and just be so in awe of the life she was blessed with. She missed John every single moment of every single day, but she always felt him with her. She never remarried or even went on a single date after he passed away. John Little was her only love. In her eyes, she remained married to him, forever and always. They say that fairy tales only exist in story books or in movies. Not this one. This one happened in real life.

This fairy tale was a little rough around the edges, and there were moments that many women would've crumbled under the weight of, but not Helen Little. Her life has been charmed. And it almost didn't happen, but it did, all because, as one little heading in the St. Louis Post-Dispatch summed it up so perfectly when their reunion at Jefferson Barracks so many years before, happened to be captured by a journalist, "Johnny Comes

Marching Home." He did indeed come marching home. And Thank God he did.

In full disclosure, I did not know what I was getting myself into in July 2017 when I attended a writer's workshop on a whim, and this thought hit me like a bolt of lightning. I am under no illusion that this work is perfect, grammatically or otherwise. I am not a professional writer—I don't pretend to be, nor do I have aspirations to be. This story wrote itself. My grandmother has had this extraordinary life, and it needed to be put on paper—through her memories and the memories of my family members and through reading every article and letter available, I was able to put this on paper. What I did not expect was the profound sadness I would feel in completing this.

As I mentioned, I did not know my grandfather as a person. The effects of his brain tumor had already taken over when I was very young. In writing this and hearing about how his personality was, seeing his own handwriting, seeing so many photos, I felt like I was meeting him for the first time. But I also had to finish the last chapter and close the book—which meant I had to say goodbye. I had to say goodbye to someone I had barely begun to get to know. Time with my grandmother is always special, because it's so precious now, but this endeavor has been an honor to go through with her. I'm simply in awe of the life she led. Thank you, Memaw, for giving me a glimpse into this time in your life. Thank you for letting me put it out there for anyone who may happen to read this. Thank you for being an amazing role model and anchor for myself and my family. I'll love you forever.

Obviously first and foremost thank you to my grandmother—for everything.

Thank you to my grandfather, Pepaw. I say that I wish you knew how amazing your wife's life continued to be after you went to Heaven, and I say that I wish you knew about all of us grandchildren and great-grandchildren—but I think you do. I think your spirit has lived on and you are very much part of this family, now and forever. Thank you for coming home.

Thank you to my mom, Susan Vickery, who provided me with so much information that she had to ask my grandmother about and relay to me since I live four hours away—thank you for getting me every piece of information right when I asked for it so the thoughts didn't leave my mind. Thank you to my aunts and uncles who talked to me about what the period of time after the war was like for my grandfather—I'm sure it isn't easy to think about or try to remember, but your help with this was invaluable and most appreciated.

Thank you to my friend Robin Young for your willingness to be an unbiased editor on this book. Your knowledge and help is greatly appreciated!

And finally, thank you to those who have served our country and continue to serve. Thank you to the families that stay behind while their loved one goes to war—you are stronger and braver than I could ever hope to be. My family was lucky enough to have my grandfather come back home—for those who did not come home, and made the ultimate sacrifice, thank you is simply not enough.

77102263R00081

Made in the USA
Lexington, KY
22 December 2017